MARTINA ET LOUIS BLÉRIOT

FERDINAND PORSCHE
PROFESSOR BEETLE

Adrien Maeght Éditeur

Only God knows
who is right and who is wrong.
F.P.

Grüß Gott!
My name is Mark Philipp Porsche.
This is the story of my great grandfather, who was a great inventor and a mechanical genius, of whom I shall tell you ...

1950

Professor Ferdinand Porsche and his son Ferry, (on the right), in the Porsche factory drawing office in Stuttgart.

Everyone has heard of Professor Porsche, but how many know that he always kept a lucky charm in his pocket in the shape of a screwdriver!

1888
Ferdinand and his family in front of their house.

He was born on September 3rd 1875 at Maffersdorf in North Bohemia. He was the third child in a family of five.

His father was a farrier.

aufgenommen April 1894
vor Abreise nach Wien

Ferdinand and the electric power generator he installed at home.

At fourteen he was apprenticed to his father. However his burning interest was in electricity.

His father returned home one evening to find that Ferdinand had installed electric lighting in the house. His father's reaction disappointed him. He advised him "to learn your trade and not waste your time with such foolishness!"

Happily his mother had faith in him. Thanks to her he was able to attend night classes at Reichenberg Technical School. In 1893 he left to take a job in the workshops of Bela Egger, who was installing electricity at Schönbrunn Castle. He continued his evening studies at the Technical High School of Vienna.

Lohner-Porsche fire engine, 1903

In 1899 he was appointed chief engineer at Lohner, a large concern making high quality horse drawn vehicles. He built within a space of only ten weeks a motor car driven by electric motors built into the front wheels and replacing horse power. It was one of the sensations at the Universal Exhibition in Paris of 1900. The huge batteries powering the electric motors were soon replaced by a Daimler petrol engine. He was awarded the Pötting prize in 1902 for this hybrid system.

Imperial manoeuvres at Sasvàr

Ferdinand Porsche driving the Cronen Prince of Austria - Hungary, Archduke Franz - Ferdinand

His Imperial and Royal Highness, the Archduke Franz-Ferdinand refers you to the recent Hungarian manoeuvres.

Both the performance of your car and your neat and skilful driving commended themselves to His Imperial and Royal Highness.

November 28th 1902

1896
Ferdinand Porsche installing an industrial electrical plant

Although he was immersed in his work of design and manufacture he managed to find time to get married. His wife Eloïse was very devoted to him and when he returned home tired out she had ready one of his favourite dishes, a goulash, washed down with Pilsen beer.

1906
A TYPE MAJA AUSTRO-DAIMLER
at Wiener Neustadt

Austro-Daimler bought the Lohner firm in 1905 and Porsche became chief engineer. The Maja was his first design. Daimlers were already building Mercedes cars at Stuttgart.

Maja and Mercedes were the names of the daughters of Emil Jellinek, the Austro-Hungarian Consul to Nice. Moving in wealthy circles on the Riviera he sold Daimlers to rich clients. He bought shares in the company and acquired exclusive sales rights for several countries. This explains how models were named after his daughters.

Eventually all Daimlers went under the name Mercedes, whilst the Maja model finished in 1909.

A racing Lohner-Porsche of 1900 with Ferdinand Porsche at the wheel!

Ferdinand Porsche was also a very capable driver. After several successful drives in Austria he took part in the Prince Henry trial which ran from Berlin to Munich through Breslau, Budapest and Salzburg. In 1909 he won "only the silver medal" but the following year the three Austro-Daimlers won most of the stages. They even reversed the headlights to make the cars more streamlined.

A 1912 Austro-Daimler aero engine
Daimler started making aero engines in 1907 and Ferdinand Porsche took part in the test flights.

In avoiding a church steeple one day too much ballast was jettisoned. The relief valve jammed and the airship kept rising and rising... There was a real danger of explosion. Luckily Porsche managed to free the valve and the "Parseval" landed!

1912, Landwehrtrain drawn by a petrol engined tractor

He built the "Landwehrtrain" for the Austrian army for moving army loads. It was a road train with a locomotive and wagons whose wheels housed electric motors. To cross a weak bridge the locomotive went first and then the wagons crossed one by one with their motors fed by a cable.
In 1916 Ferdinand Porsche received the highest honour for a civilian, becoming an officer of the Order of Franz-Josef.

Austro-Daimler Type M-17
1914

Ferry Porsche had inherited his father's interests and yearned to have his own car... a dream which came true in 1920, when he found under the Christmas tree a superb miniature car built by his father.
 Ferdinand was amazed when his son, unaided, started it up and roared off. He had taught himself to drive by moving cars around in the Daimler works...

Targa Florio 19..
Austro-Daimler Type ADS R. (Sascha)

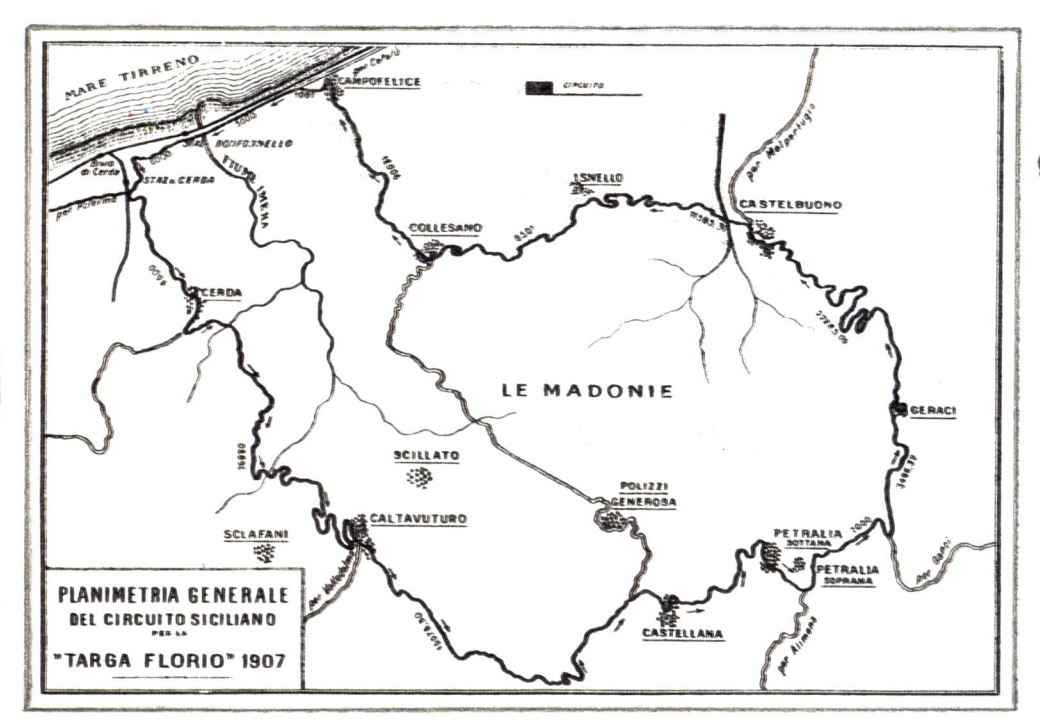

The little racing Sascha built by Porsche in 1922 was the sensation of the Targa Florio in Sicily that year. Vincenzo Florio founded the race, over earth roads in the north of Sicily in 1906. Over the years the distance covered varied between 4 and 10 laps of the 148 kilometre circuit. The starting point was Cerda.

To start with it was almost a social event to promote a fashionable aperitif. Gradually it became an important event. It was not held during the two World Wars, but qualified as a World Championship race from 1955 to 1973. Following an accident in which two spectators were killed, 1977 was the last year.

1927, Otto Merz wins at the Nürburgring in an SSK Mercedes, one of the famous family of S, SS, SSK and SSKL models

After the Sascha Porsche designed for Austro-Daimler, which he quit in 1923, the very successful ADM model. He then became technical director at Daimlers in Stuttgart, but still crawled underneath the cars! After Christian Werner's 1924 win in the Targa Florio driving the successful supercharged 2 litre Mercedes he was given the title of Dr. Ing. h.c. by Stuttgart University – he had held that of Dr. Ing. h.c. of Vienna since 1917. Up to the expiry of his contract with Daimler in 1928 he designed touring cars, lorries and aviation engines.

1929 - Steyr Type XXX

For a year he applied his expertise with the Austrian firm of Steyr. He then founded, in 1931 with his son in law Dr. Anton Piëch, his own firm, a design centre for road vehicles, aircraft and boats.
His son Ferry started working with him as did his nephew Ghislain Kaes.
He first designed several cars for Wanderer, and then had orders from Zündapp and NSU, both motorcycle makers who wanted to sell small cars because of falling motorcycle sales. By the time the prototypes were ready, the motorcycle market had picked up...

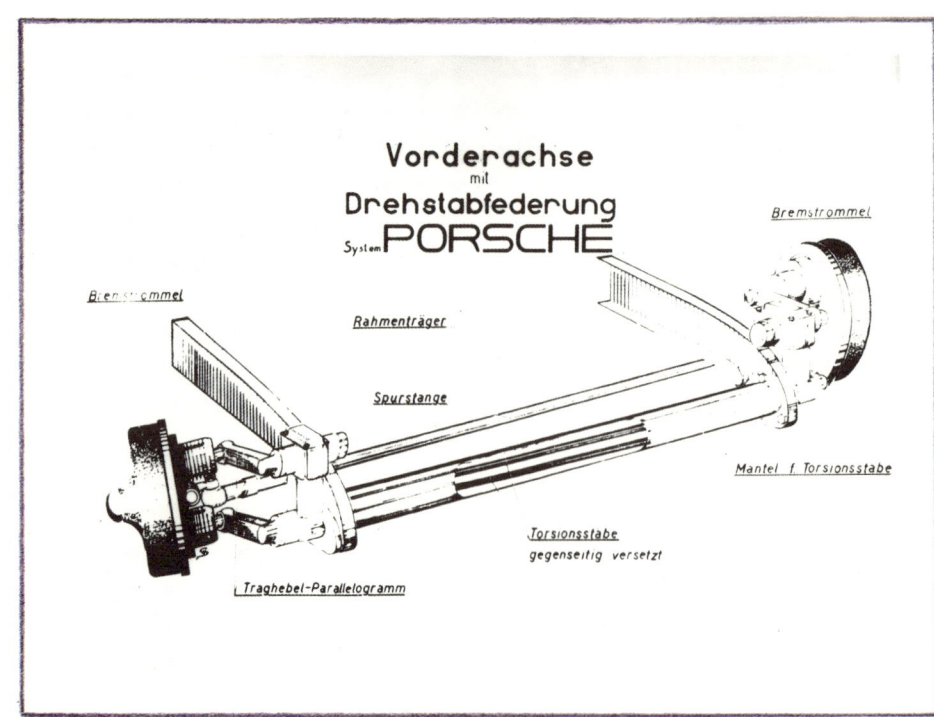

1931

The Russian government was impressed by Porsche's inventiveness and in 1932 invited him to Moscow.
He was shown round various establishments in the capital and then taken to an enormous tractor factory in Stalingrad.
Finally he was offered the position of "Director General in charge of construction and development of the Russian motor industry".
But Porsche refused... he was too old to start a new life in a foreign country, and above all he neither spoke nor understood Russian, which would have posed problems on the technical side

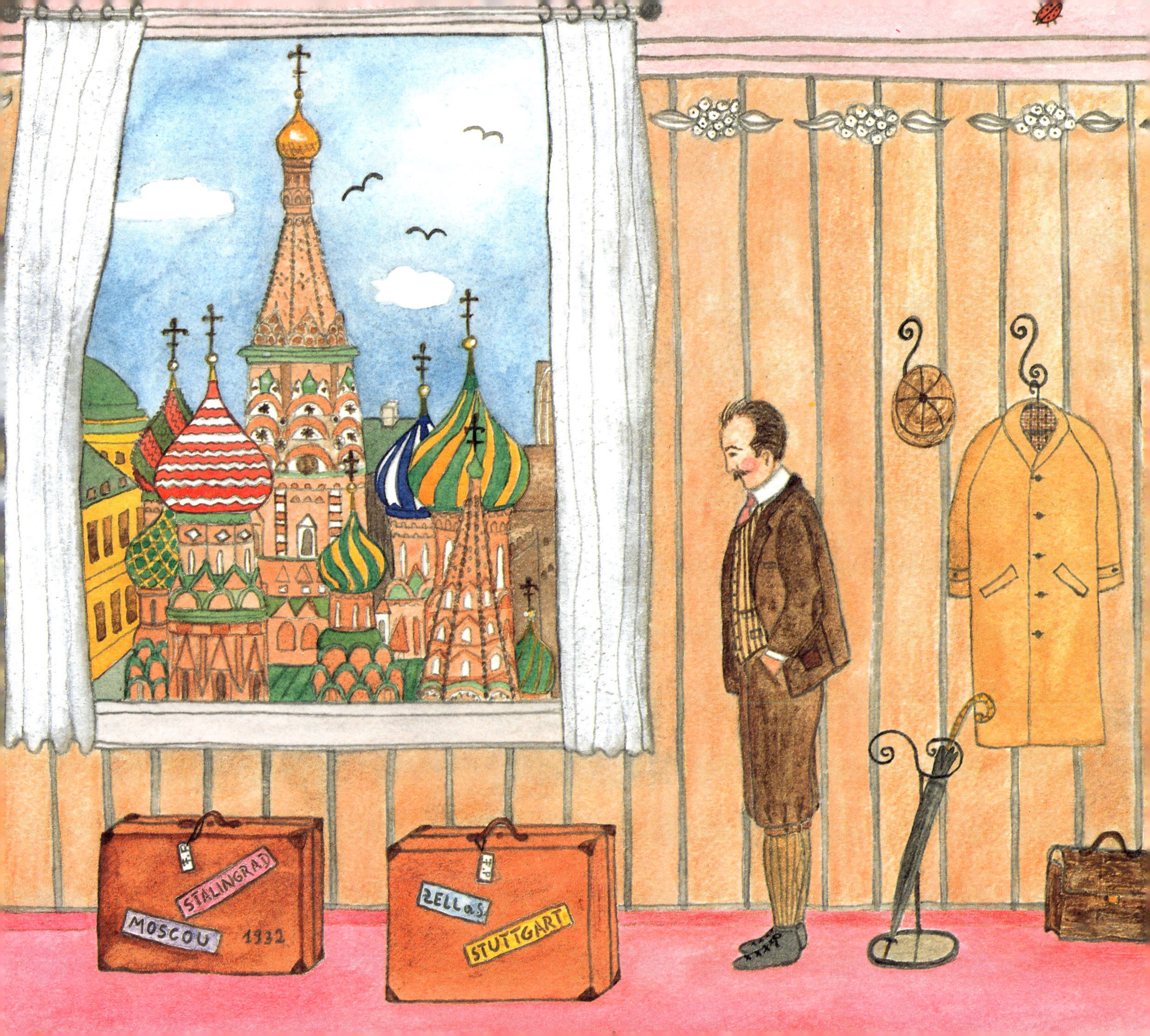
STALINGRAD
MOSCOU
1932
ZELLaS.
STUTTGART

1936
Bernd Rosemeyer wins the German Grand Prix
AUTO UNION

1934   1935   1936

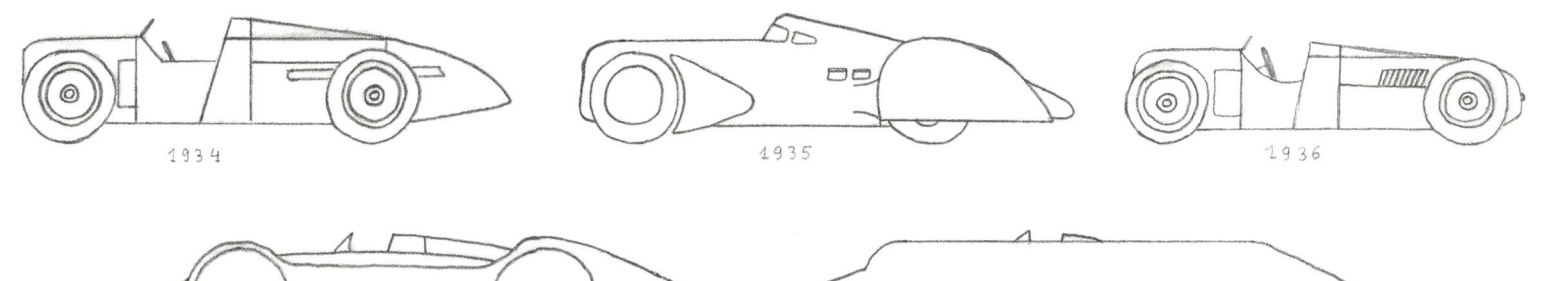

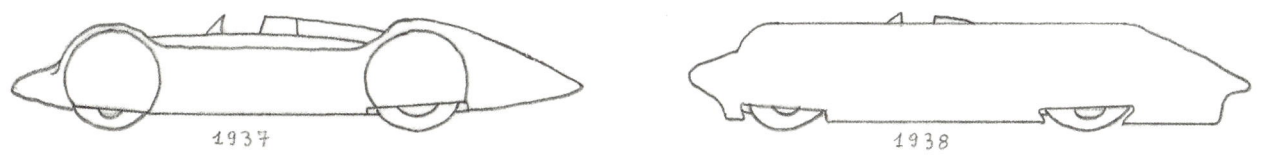

1937   1938

Hitler, who assumed power in 1933, decided to donate money towards building a racing car in order to display Germany's technical prowess.

Both Daimler-Benz[1] and Auto-Union (an amalgamation of Audi, Horch, DKW and Wanderer) were given funds to design a prototype.

Porsche, who already had plans for a revolutionary racing car, signed a contract with Auto-Union.

The first racing Auto-Union had a 4 litre 16 cylinder engine. It was mounted behind the driver and gave off 250 horsepower. During its first race in 1934 on the Avus circuit at Berlin it beat a world speed record at 135 mph, driven by Hans Stuck.

Together with the Mercedes the Auto-Unions dominated international racing, gaining many successes finally giving off 600 h.p.

[1] Daimler and Benz merged in 1926.

VW 30, 1937
985 cc air cooled flat four cylinder engine with torsion bar suspension.

Hitler had asked the car makers every year since 1934 at the Annual Berlin Motor Show to produce a peoples car (in German: "Volks-wagen"). It was to be simple, economical, reliable, a four or five seater, reach 60 m.p.h. and do over 30 miles per gallon... and cost no more than a motorcycle.

Luckily Porsche had kept the designs he had drawn up for NSU

Type 110 "Volksschlepper" 1938.
A lightweight farm tractor with an air cooled diesel engine
It was economical and adaptable to varied uses and was
to be mass produced in a specially built factory.
The war stopped this project.

and Zündapp and sent them to the Ministry for Industry. With Hitler's approval Porsche signed a contract on June 22nd 1934 with the German Motor Industry Federation (RDA) to make the Volkswagen.

Helped by a team of a dozen the first three prototypes - called VW 3 - were built locally in the villa Porsche Feuerbacher-weg at Stuttgart.

After they were completed in October 1936 the VW 3's were thoroughly tested by experts from the RDA. Each car had to cover 30,000 miles. Ferry, newly married and a young father, spent many hours behind the wheel. On their successful conclusion a run of 30 cars - VW 30 - later raised to 60 - VW 60 - was made by Mercedes Benz and given a 50,000 mile test during 1937 and 1938.

In the meantime Porsche, together with a group of his engineers, including Ferry, went to America to study mass production methods. They also met Henry Ford, and placed orders for machinery to install in the giant new Volkswagen factory with its 4000 foot frontage! This was being built at Fallersleben in Lower Saxony, on ground belonging to the Count von der Schulenburg.

On his return he was awarded the German National Prize which entitled him to the style of Professor Honoris Causa.

A new town to house the thousands of workers was also built on the site. The factory was meant to start production in October 1939 but unfortunately war broke out the month before.

Prototype Porsche Daimler T 80, 1938

This was a six wheeled record breaker whose trials were interrupted by the war. It didn't have a gearbox, merely a clutch. It was necessary either to push or tow it to start...

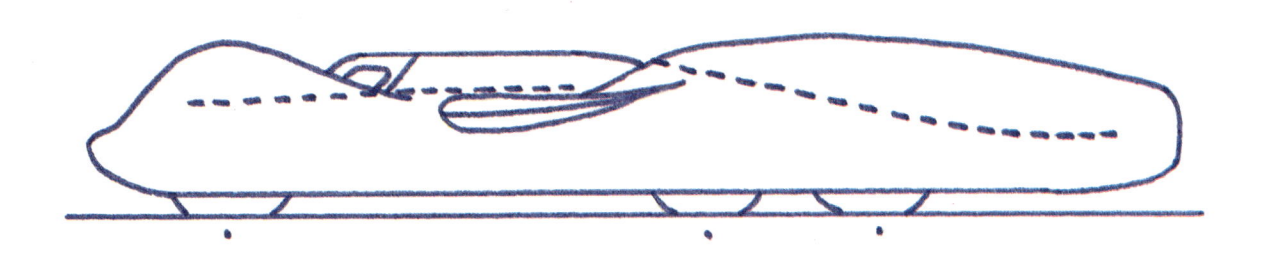

Bodywork: duralumin and removable
Length: 27' 6"
Weight: 2,6 tons
12 cylinder V type aircraft engine of 44,7 litres capacity
Power: 3030 bhp.
Max. Speed: 400 mph.

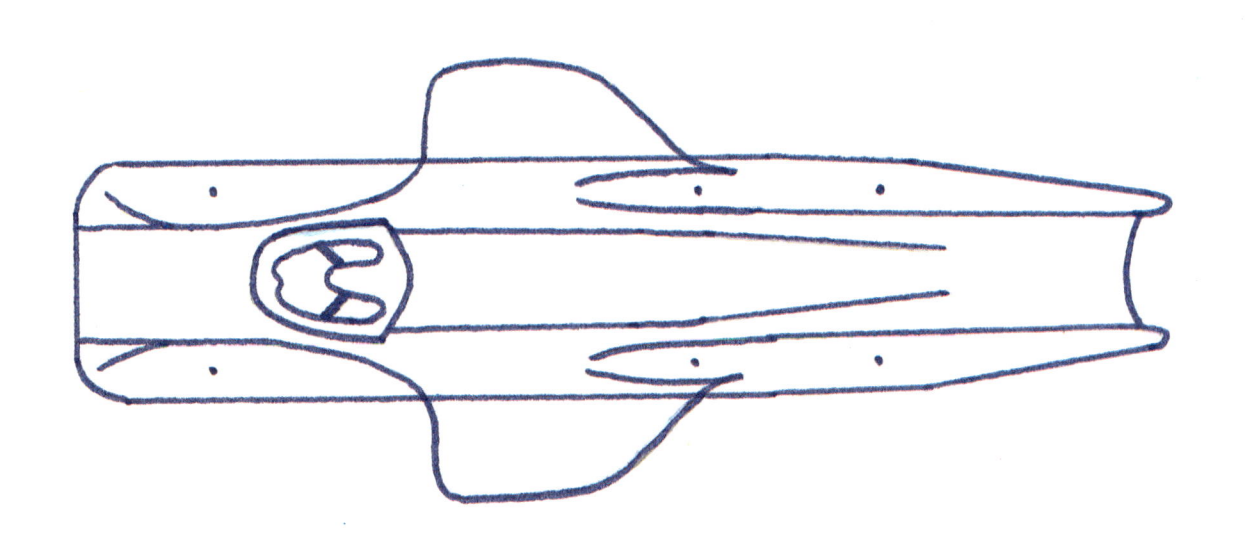

Porsche Schwimmwagen 1942
Type 166
With all four wheels driving it was capable of climbing 65° slopes. It could do 7 mph in water and 50 mph on roads.

Now the Volkswagen factory was making military equipment. Within a few months a cross country military version of the Volkswagen appeared. Light and strong this car, called "Kübelwagen", saw service on all fronts, from North Africa to Russia in the years 1940 to 1945. Reliable and easily maintained a total of 50.435 were made.
An amphibious version called the "Schwimmwagen" was introduced in 1942 and 14.283 were built. It was one of the best cross country vehicles of the war. Ferry Porsche was responsible for making these two versions.

1942, the windmill

In 1940 the Porsche design office was directed to tank design. Their first model (Type 100), the "Leopard" of 35 tons re-adopted the mixed diesel-lectric system. It was followed by the 59 ton "Tiger" (Type 101) of which 3 were made in 1942, and in turn by the Type 130 "Ferdinand" or "Elephant", a tank destroyer of which 100 were built.
The most extraordinary tank however was the Type 205 "Maus" (Mouse). This was the biggest tank ever made, weighing 188 tons and armed with a 150 m/m gun. Its development was halted by the ending of hostilities.

The four wheel driving Type 360 racing car with a flat twelve cylinder engine of 1500 cc developing 360 bhp.

Due to the bombing of Stuttgart the Porsche design office moved to Gmünd in Carinthia (Austria) in the autumn of 1944.

The end of the war found the Volkswagen factory two thirds destroyed and Porsche and his son imprisoned in Baden-Baden. Ferry was released after some months, but his father ended up in a French prison. He was initially housed in a maidservant's room in Renault's villa in Paris, where he was ordered to examine and progress the plans for the new 4 CV car.

He was then transferred to an unheated prison at Dijon, where his health worsened. When he was found innocent of the false accusations levelled against him he was released in August 1947 on payment of a million franc fine.

Ferry managed to raise this money by signing a contract with an Italian industrialist, Pietro Susio, to design the CISITALIA Formula 1 car.

When Ferdinand Porsche finally returned home after two years in captivity and looked at the drawings, he said "Its exactly as I would have designed it myself".

Although the Cisitalia was a very advanced design at the time, it never raced, since by the time it had been built the Formula 1 regulations had been changed by barring supercharged cars.

Type 114

10 cylinder Vee type located between driver and rear axle
1500 cc
water cooled
Only a wind tunnel model was built

Type 60 K 10

Uprated Volkswagen engine of 1131 cc
Power: 40 bhp (nearly twice that of standard engine)
Streamlined aluminium bodywork
Speed: 82 mph
3 vehicles built

The idea of a Porsche sports car stemmed from the Type 114 of 1938 and above all with the Type 60 K 10 which was destined for the BERLIN-ROME race of September 1939, cancelled because of the war...

... It wasn't until June 8th 1948 that the dream was realised with the birth of the Type 356, the first car to be called a Porsche! Two Porsche 356's were exhibited at the Geneva Motor show in 1949, and a further fifty were built by hand in a year at Gmünd. In September 1949 Porsche settled in Stuttgart. Production of 500 cars was anticipated but in fact 78.000 Porsche 356's were finally built!

Ferdinand and Eloïse Porsche with their grandchildren

Sadly Professor Porsche died on January 30th 1951 at Stuttgart following a stroke. Despite this sad blow, production continued in the factory. Soon after preparations began for the Le Mans 24 hour race. A Porsche driven by Auguste Veuillet and Edmond Mouche won the 1100 cc category.

Porsche 911

6 cylinder 1991 cc. 130 bhp. engine, 130 mph

Ferry Porsche's eldest son, Ferdinand Alexander Porsche, now head of PORSCHE DESIGN, was the designer in 1961 of the 911.

This superseded the 356 in 1964 and was made in several versions such as 911S, Targa, Carrera...

At the end of a life devoted to designing other people's cars this victory finally established the Porsche name, for so long linked to the history of the motor car.

Under the inspired leadership of Ferry Porsche the firm gained countless victories in competition, becoming a legend amongst racing and sports cars.

The Volkswagen factory at Wolfsburg (renamed in 1945) was rebuilt after the war and finally started making the Beetle seven years after the original planned date.

After a shaky start production built up rapidly. After Heinz Nordhoff was made chief in 1948 the Beetle swamped the world and became the best selling car of all time with more than 20.000.000 built by 1981 after 45 years of production.

END

Acknowledgment for their valuable help we wish to thank:

    Hofrat Dr Karl Gaisbacher
    Prof. Dipl. Ing. Helmut Gilli
    Ing. Richard v. Kaan
    Rosemarie Moser
    Klaus Parr
    Dr Ing. H.C. Ferry Porsche, Porsche AG Zuffenhausen
    F.A. Porsche, Porsche Design, Zell am See
    Hubertus Schröder
    Jens Sochor
    Volkswagen AG Wolfsburg

Bibliography :

    « L'Automobiliste » n° 68, 71/72, Adrien Maeght Éditeur
    J. Bentley/F. Porsche : « Ein Traum wird Wirklichkeit », Econit
    R.V. Frankenberg : « Histoire des grandes marques », Marabout
    Karl Ludvigsen : « Porsche, Geschichte und Technik der Renn
        und Sportwagen », BLV München
    W. Oswald : « Kraftfahrzeuge und Panzer der Reichswehr
        Wehrmacht und Bundeswehr », Motorbuchverlag
    J. Piekalkiewicz : « Der VW Kübelwagen Typ 82 », Motorbuchverlag
    Saint-Loup : « Dix millions de Coccinelles », Presses de la Cité
    J.-P. Thévoz : « Les Automobiles célèbres de l'histoire », Ed. 24 Heures

by the same authors: "Destination? Dover!"
"Roland Garros, roi des airs"

Drawings by Martina Blériot
printed by Arte Adrien Maeght - Paris.
November 1990

© Adrien Maeght Éditeur 1989

ISBN 2-86941-134-0